W9-BNF-730

Dress Codes in Schools

Other books in the Issues That Concern You series:

Dress Codes in Schools

Jill Hamilton, *Book Editor*

GREENHAVEN PRESS
A part of Gale, Cengage Learning

GALE
CENGAGE Learning™

Detroit • New York • San Francisco • New Haven, Conn • Waterville, Maine • London

Christine Nasso, *Publisher*
Elizabeth Des Chenes, *Managing Editor*

For more information, contact:
Greenhaven Press
27500 Drake Rd.
Farmington Hills, MI 48331-3535
Or you can visit our Internet site at gale.cengage.com

LIBRARY OF CONGRESS CATALOGING-IN-PUBLICATION DATA

Dress codes in schools / Jill Hamilton, book editor.
p. cm. — (Issues that concern you)
Includes bibliographical references and index.
ISBN-13: 978-0-7377-3984-8 (hardcover)
1. Students—United States—Uniforms. 2. Dress codes—United States. I. Hamilton, Jill.
LB3024.D743 2008
371.51—dc22

2008002941

Printed in the United States of America
2 3 4 5 6 7 12 11 10 09 08

CONTENTS

Appendix

Long Beach Unified School District: A Uniform Success Story?

Each fall when another school year begins, more students find themselves faced with new dress codes or uniform policies. The dress codes are becoming more popular around the country as school officials credit them with doing everything from creating a more professional learning environment to reducing gang activity.

Although President Bill Clinton gave a boost to school uniforms by recommending them in his 1996 State of the Union address, it was the pioneering efforts of the Long Beach Unified School District (LBUSD) that first set the trend in motion. In 1994 the California city became the first large urban school district to institute a uniform policy. Long Beach is on the California coast, but it does not fit the stereotype of a Southern California beach town. Although the city boasts an impressive downtown and areas of expensive homes, nearly one-fifth of the residents live below the federal poverty line. The poverty and its accompanying problems of gang activities and underachievement were some of the reasons that Long Beach opted to try a school uniform policy.

The following year, in 1995, the district came out with some startling data. According to the district's research, uniforms had had a huge effect on crime and disciplinary problems. Fighting was down 51 percent, drug use was down 69 percent, and sex offenses were down 74 percent. By contrast, during the same period, crime in the district's high schools, where uniforms were not required, increased 28 percent. In schools that adopted the policy, every measurable criminal activity was down, regardless of whether the school was in a poor neighborhood or a wealthy one. The uniforms were also popular in the community. A 1994 survey by the *Long Beach Press-Telegram*, the local paper, showed more than 80 percent of readers supported the policy. And a 1995 survey by LBUSD showed that 91 percent of parents agreed that school uniforms improve the school environment.

The apparent success of LBUSD's uniform policy has continued. The district extended the policy to include two major high schools, and now about seventy-two thousand Long Beach students head to class in uniform. Under California law parents can request an exemption from school uniforms, but each year only about 2 percent make that request. In 2003 LBUSD won the Broad Prize for Urban Education and was a finalist for the award in 2007.

Schools everywhere have experimented with the use of dress codes, with varying results.

The award honors urban school districts that show the greatest overall improvement in student achievement while reducing achievement gaps for disadvantaged students. In 2007 test scores for Long Beach elementary students beat others in the state, and in the same year Long Beach student achievement was cited in a report called *Beating the Odds* by Council of the Great City Schools.

Thirteen years after it was implemented, LBUSD's uniform policy appeared to be a great success. Still, not everyone agreed that it was the uniforms that helped to improve Long Beach schools. In their influential study, "Effects of Student Uniforms on Attendance, Behavior Problems, Substance Abuse, and Academic Achievement," David L. Brunsma and Kerry A. Rockquemore examined existing data and determined that uniforms did not lead to an improvement in attendance, behavior, drug use, or academic achievement. Other research notes that the gains may be due to better teaching methods, more effective discipline, and a greater focus on test preparation. And some worry that school districts are relying on dress codes as a panacea for schools while ignoring deeper problems.

For its part, Long Beach has done its best to make uniforms more palatable to students and parents. Although colors of tops and bottoms are limited, students are free to choose from a variety of styles. Large chain stores, realizing that school uniforms are big business, have started offering more fashionable styles that stay within the guidelines. High school and middle school students get an additional color for pants and skirts, thus giving them a way to differentiate themselves from younger students. For parents who worry about the cost of uniforms, the district and local charities offer free or reduced-cost uniforms. As the district is careful to note, three uniforms cost about the same as one pair of designer jeans. But perhaps the best indicator of the uniform policy's success was that when the policy was extended to the two large high schools, there was no major effort by parents or students to fight the change.

In the rest of the country the issue is still up for debate. In this anthology authors, including parents, teachers, and school administrators, debate the various aspects of the discussion, including whether dress codes stifle individuality, dress codes vs. uniforms,

The use of dress codes is a much-disputed issue for students, teachers, administrators, and parents.

whether teachers should have dress codes, and other timely top-ics. In addition, there are several appendixes for readers who are interested in further exploring the topic. "What You Should Know About Dress Codes in Schools" gives readers a quick, bulleted look at pertinent facts about the issue. "What You Should Do About Dress Codes in Schools" offers concrete advice for those who are interested in fighting—or starting—a dress code policy. The appen-dixes also include an extensive bibliography of media sources and a list of organizations to contact. *Issues That Concern You: Dress Codes in Schools*, offers a wide-ranging look at the current issues on this topic.

ONE

The Debate over Dress Codes and Uniforms

Marian Wilde

> The following viewpoint provides an overview of the debate over school dress codes and uniforms. Author Marian Wilde discusses the difference between dress codes and school uniforms and offers sample policies for each. She also gives the pro and con arguments on school uniforms and provides a comparison of dress codes vs. uniforms. Wilde also reports on the studies on the effects of school dress codes and how educators have reacted to the research. Wilde is a staff writer for GreatSchools.net.

Recent data indicates that 23% of public elementary schools in the U.S. have a school uniform policy, but a new book makes the case that uniforms do not improve school safety or academic discipline.

Why Do Some Public Schools Have Uniforms?

In the 1980s, public schools were often compared unfavorably to Catholic schools. Noting the perceived benefit that uniforms conferred upon Catholic schools, some public schools decided to adopt a school uniform policy.

President [Bill] Clinton provided momentum to the school uniform movement when he said in his 1996 State of the Union

Marian Wilde, "The Debate over Dress Codes and Uniforms," *GreatSchools*, July 2006. www.greatschools.net. Reproduced by permission.

speech, "If it means that teenagers will stop killing each other over designer jackets, then our public schools should be able to require their students to wear school uniforms."

What Studies Say About School Uniforms

University of Missouri assistant professor David Brunsma had a different reaction to President Clinton's remark. He decided that some scientific methodology was in order. In a 2004 book, *The School Uniform Movement and What It Tells Us About American Education: A Symbolic Crusade*, Brunsma offers a comprehensive look at the studies conducted to date on the effect of uniforms on academic performance.

Brunsma also analyzed two enormous databases, the 1988 National Educational Longitudinal Study and the 1998 Early Childhood Longitudinal Study, and found no positive correlation between uniforms and school safety and academic achievement.

"I'm generalizing here," says Brunsma,

> but by and large I feel a stronger sense of support and understanding of the results from teachers who are on the ground working through these issues on a daily basis. However, administrators (principals and board members) seem to have more of a problem with the results and arguments presented across my body of work and the work of others who study this issue. Administrators appear to want to continue relying on anecdotal aspects of the debate while simply disregarding rigorous, scientific study of the issue.

The school uniform movement has now spread to about a quarter of all public elementary schools. Experts say that the number of middle and high schools with uniforms is about half the number of elementary schools.

Why, if uniforms are intended to curb school violence and improve academics, are they not more prevalent in middle and high schools, where these goals are just as important as they are in elementary schools? Because, notes Brunsma, "It's desperately much more difficult to implement uniforms in high schools, and even middle schools, for the student resistance is much, much higher. In fact, most of the

Nine-year-old Arielle Mendoza is fitted by teacher Shelley Moreno at a Wal-Mart in San Antonio. Hundreds of Wal-Mart stores are now stocking school uniforms.

litigation resulting from uniforms has been located at levels of K-12 that are higher than elementary schools. Of course, this uniform debate is also one regarding whether children have rights, too!"

The Pros and Cons of School Uniforms

According to proponents, school uniforms:

- Help prevent gangs from forming on campus
- Encourage discipline
- Help students resist peer pressure to buy trendy clothes
- Help identify intruders in the school
- Diminish economic and social barriers between students
- Increase a sense of belonging and school pride
- Improve attendance

Opponents contend that school uniforms:
- Violate a student's right to freedom of expression
- Are simply a Band-Aid on the issue of school violence
- Make students a target for bullies from other schools
- Are a financial burden for poor families
- Are an unfair additional expense for parents who pay taxes for a free public education
- Are difficult to enforce in public schools

Uniforms vs. Dress Codes
Schools and districts differ widely in how closely they adhere to the concept of uniformity.

A Uniform Policy in Baltimore, Maryland

Type:	Voluntary uniform policy at Mt. Royal Elementary/Middle School
Opt-out:	Uniforms are voluntary
Size of program:	950 elementary and middle school students
Implementation date:	1989

Support for Disadvantaged Students:

Mt. Royal Elementary/Middle School keeps a store of uniforms that are provided free to students who cannot afford the $35.00 to purchase them. Ninety-eight percent of graduating eighth graders donate their uniforms to the school.

Results:

According to Mt. Royal's assistant principal, Rhonda Thompson, the uniform policy "has enhanced the tone and climate of our building. It brings about a sense of seriousness about work." All of the students have elected to participate in the uniform program.

Taken from: U.S. Department of Education.

What's a uniform? One school might require white button-down shirts and ties for boys and pleated skirts for girls and blazers adorned with the school logo for all. Another school may simply require that all shirts have collars. In Toledo, Ohio, for example, elementary school students have a limited palette of colors that they can wear: white, light blue, dark blue or yellow on the top half and dark blue, navy, khaki or tan on the bottom half.

Toledo girls are allowed a fairly wide range of dress items, however: blouses, polo shirts with collars, turtlenecks, skirts, jumpers, slacks, and knee-length shorts and skirts. Boys have almost as many choices: dress shirts, turtlenecks, polo or button-down shirts, pants or knee-length shorts. And when these Toledo kids reach junior high, they are treated to one more color choice: maroon.

What's a dress code? Dress codes are less restrictive than uniform policies. They usually focus on promoting modesty and discouraging anti-social fashion statements.

In Tulsa, Oklahoma, the public schools have a fairly specific dress code. Among many other items, their code prohibits:

- Decorations (including tattoos) that are symbols, mottoes, words or acronyms that convey crude, vulgar, profane, violent, gang-related, sexually explicit or suggestive messages
- Large or baggy clothes
- Holes in clothes
- Scarves, curlers, bandanas or sweatbands inside of school buildings (Exceptions are made for religious attire.)
- Visible undergarments
- Strapless garments
- Bare midriffs, immodestly low cut necklines or bare backs
- Tights, leggings, bike shorts, swim suits or pajamas as outerwear
- Visible piercings, except in the ear
- Dog collars, tongue rings and studs, wallet chains, large hair picks, or chains that connect one part of the body to another

Changes in Dress Codes

If a school principal from the 1960s—when the prime concern was that skirts reached to the knees—were to visit a school today, he might wonder at our current attitudes.

Today, principals have bigger concerns than exposed knees, such as exposed stomachs, backs and cleavage—risqué styles that originated with such pop stars as Madonna, Jennifer Lopez and Britney Spears.

The newest trend, in the world of school dress codes, is mounting pressure to establish dress codes for teachers. Apparently the same casual mind-set toward revealing outfits is cropping up in the ranks of our teachers.

It's a Big Issue

The debate over uniforms in the public schools encompasses many larger issues than simply what your child should wear to school. It touches on issues of school improvement, freedom of expression and the "culture wars." It's no wonder the debate rages on.

TWO

Students Can Fight Dress Codes

Marisa Kakoulas

> The following viewpoint was written by Marisa Kakoulas to help students and parents who want to fight "oppressive" school dress codes. Kakoulas, a corporate consultant and lawyer who is also interested in tattoos and other body modification issues, cites previous cases involving dress code issues and interprets what they could mean for other cases. She provides a list of facts to know about dress codes and offers specific advice regarding the issues of tattoos, piercings, and hair color. Kakoulas writes a legal column for *BMEzine*, a publication about body modification.

"It can hardly be argued that either students or teachers shed their rights at the schoolhouse gate. . . . In our system, state-operated schools may not be the enclaves of totalitarianism. School officials do not possess absolute authority over their students. . . ."

With these words, US Supreme Court Justice Abe Fortas gave students the right to freedom of speech in the landmark case of *Tinker v. Des Moines Independent Community School District* decided in 1969.

The Supreme Court didn't consider this right absolute and said that expression could be limited if it constitutes a foreseeable substantial disruption or material interference with school activities. But overall, it established the principle that a student's appearance falls under First Amendment protection.

The *Tinker* case involved students who wore black armbands to protest the Vietnam war, but even today has been cited in cases involving student hair color, piercings, and tattoos. It is this case, as well as many others, that has been proven an excellent weapon in the fight against oppressive school dress policies. Facts, knowledge of the law, and the threat of monetary damages are all part of the arsenal. (Honor Roll also helps.) If you're going to do battle, either for yourself, on behalf of your child or even as a concerned citizen, educate yourself first.

Arm Yourself with the Facts

- In the US, the State, not the feds, regulate school dress codes and uniforms.
- So far, no state legislature has mandated its public schools to set out dress codes or uniforms, although many states have enacted legislation that addresses the issue.
- Local school boards are often the bodies that decide on what is appropriate dress in school and then have the schools themselves enforce their codes.
- School board officials are mainly elected. People who share your ideology can be voted in. Those who oppose can be voted out.
- Many school board officials throughout the country have cited that uniforms and strict dress codes are used to combat crime and disciplinary problems in schools.
- However, requiring students to wear uniforms has had no direct effect on drug abuse, behavioral problems or school attendance, according to a 1998 study entitled "The Effects of Student Uniforms on Attendance, Behavioral Problems, Substance Abuse, and Academic Achievement" published in *The Journal of Educational Research*.

- The study went on to say: "Students wearing uniforms did not appear to have any significantly different academic preparedness, proschool attitudes, or peer group structures with proschool attitudes than other students." In other words, uniforms do not lead to good behavior.

Knowing the basic facts about dress codes and uniforms is only your first line of attack. If you or your child is threatened with suspension or dismissal because of appearance, find support in the law.

Aimee Scarduzio and her mother Sherry were among the plaintiffs who challenged the Waterbury (Connecticut) Public Schools dress code in 1999, when a judge ruled that students did not have a constitutional right to wear baggy jeans that could conceal weapons.

Cries for fairness and the need for students to express themselves make for great protest slogans, but law suits often get better results. It may not be pretty, but it's the American way.

Some student challenges to dress codes have met with great success and others left the students expelled with no further recourse but to change schools. There are no easy ways to predict how courts may rule either. For instance, the courts have ruled differently for different body modifications and have often hinged on just certain facts.

Dress Codes and Tattoos

A good example of how courts have dealt with dress codes and tattoos is *Stephenson v. Davenport Community School District* decided in 1997. The case involved a high school honor roll student, Brianna Stephenson, who self-poked a small cross tattoo on her hand two years before school administrators took notice of it. The school had enacted a new code that said "gang-related activities such as display of 'colors', symbols, signs, etc. will not be tolerated on school grounds." They deemed Brianna's tattoo to be a gang symbol, which she denied. Nevertheless, the school set a deadline for Brianna to remove the tattoo or face disciplinary action. Brianna complied and underwent painful and expensive laser treatments that burned off layers of skin on her hand and left a scar.

When Brianna returned to school, she sued the school district for monetary damages claiming that the district violated her First Amendment rights by forcing her to remove the tattoo. The United States District Court dismissed her case, but the U.S. Court of Appeals for the Eighth Circuit granted her appeal.

The Eighth Circuit found in favor of Brianna and ruled that the school district's policy was unconstitutional because it was too vague. According to the Court, the policy did not give students enough information about exactly what kind of conduct and expression was prohibited. The vague regulation also allowed for arbitrary or discriminatory enforcement. The school could find the tattoo cross on Brianna to be a threat while on another student they could deem it a sign of devout faith.

After the school district paid out, they changed the policy. But it was not a great victory for tattooed students. If the policy was not vague and was clear on what forms of expression were banned, would Brianna still have won? It is unclear, although some legal scholars say yes, particularly after recent rulings in Massachusetts and South Carolina deeming tattoo art as an accepted form of symbolic speech. In the October 2000 case that struck down a 38-year old ban on tattooing in Massachusetts, Judge Barbara Rouse stated: "Persons obtain tattoos to demonstrate commitment to other persons, to institutions, to religious beliefs, and to political and personal beliefs. The medium on which the drawn image appears should not be relevant when determining whether something is 'speech'; the tattoo itself is symbolic speech deserving of First Amendment protection."

Dress Codes and Piercings

Students with piercings have not fared as well in the courts, however. For example, when an Illinois school district banned male students from wearing earrings in an effort to combat gang presence in the school, the courts upheld the policy stating that the male student's rights to freedom of expression were not violated because their message was one of individuality, a message that is not protected under the First Amendment.

Other courts have cited the need for students to act in accordance with "community standards" and have upheld dress codes that ban piercings in an effort to prevent disrespect for authority and discipline. Piercings have also been deemed a health and safety hazard that schools have a right to govern.

Nevertheless, dress codes banning piercings can still be fought, but require a united front of parents and students working together. A little help from the American Civil Liberties Union (ACLU) is also a plus.

When Julie Cahill, an 18-year-old Rhode Island high school honor student was banned from mentoring elementary students because of her lip ring and purple hair, the ACLU stepped in and put pressure on the school committee. Steven Brown, Executive

Director of the ACLU's Rhode Island chapter, said in a letter to the school:

> Surely it is no secret that role models come in all shapes, sizes, styles and even hair colors. As Cahill's résumé so obviously shows, people with purple or pink hair, no less than blondes, can be excellent mentors to young kids. At the same time, drug treatment facilities are filled with natural brunettes. Indeed, having a person who chooses to look different might even teach young kids a thing or two about resisting peer pressure—one of the most potent promoters of drug use and poor decision-making.

The school responded by saying that, unlike the immutable characteristic of, say, skin color, Julie is free to remove the dye from her

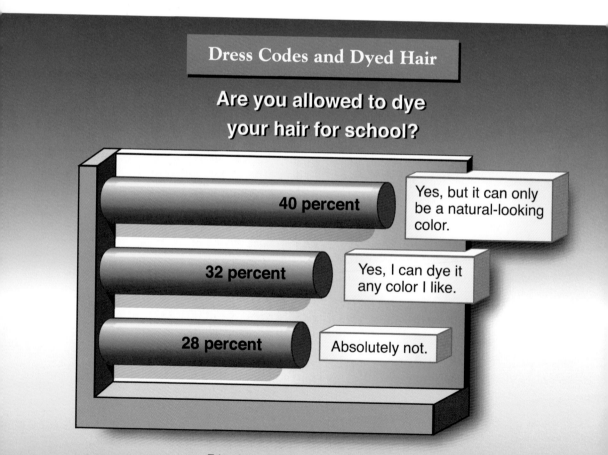

Dress Codes and Dyed Hair

Are you allowed to dye your hair for school?

40 percent — Yes, but it can only be a natural-looking color.

32 percent — Yes, I can dye it any color I like.

28 percent — Absolutely not.

Taken from: "Gothic Schoolgirls," Mister Poll.

hair and the ring from her lip. To which the ACLU replied, "Discrimination against blacks is not wrong because they can't help being black—it is wrong because it treats a person unfairly on the basis of a totally irrelevant characteristic." Powerful words to keep in mind when defending your own right to modify your body.

Dress Codes and Hair Color
The ACLU has gotten behind a number of hair color cases and won. For example, the ACLU of Virginia won a $25,000 award in legal fees against a school board that suspended a student for coloring his hair blue. The district court's decision in that case was based on a 1972 Fourth Circuit Court of Appeals ruling, *Massie v. Henry*, holding that students have a "right to wear their hair as they wish as an aspect of the right to be secure in one's person guaranteed by the due process clause." However, in many instances these cases do not make it to court as the schools tend to reinstate the multicolored-haired students once the ACLU intervenes.

What is also interesting is that often those students that win their battles against restrictive dress codes are those that have excellent academic records. The ACLU's press releases on student appearance cases are filled with the words "honor roll" and "model student." In school, as in life in general, personal excellence has the ability to break down walls of appearance-based discrimination.

THREE

Enforcement of Dress Codes Wastes Time

Kathleen Modenbach

Kathleen Modenbach, a teacher in a school with a uniform policy, was secretly amused to note that no matter what her school's dress code rules were, the students could find ways around them. One student interpreted a rule that students could wear sport coats as an invitation to wear a loud, 1950's-style plaid jacket adorned with buttons. Other students usurped a rule that dictated hair length by shaping their hair into brightly colored spikes. In Modenbach's opinion, trying to keep up with this is "a waste of time" for school administrators and teachers. "Let's just focus our energy on teaching them," she writes.

William sat in the last row of one of my English IV classes last year [2001]. He came to our school from England at just about the time school uniforms became mandatory for our students. Smart, quiet, and a bit counter-culture, William liked art, literature, and—most of all—his unique identity!

I knew that William and the uniform code would clash, but he wasn't the type to express his displeasure in a loud manner. Instead, every day, William wore a very '50s sport coat. The regulations permitted sport coats as long as the uniform was visible underneath,

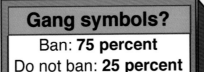

Kids Vote on What Is Okay to Wear to School

Gang symbols?

Ban: **75 percent**
Do not ban: **25 percent**

Leila Haydari, sixteen, of Benicia, California, says a school security guard made her take off her bandanna because he thought it could be mistaken for a gang symbol. (It was not.)

Baggy clothes?

Ban: **19 percent**
Do not ban: **81 percent**

Says Bryan Carver, thirteen, of Madison, Connecticut: "I'm a skater, so I'm into baggy clothes." But not at school.

Uniforms?

Pro: **17 percent**
Anti: **83 percent**

"For me, uniforms are not a problem," says Josah Drimi, seventeen, of Mercy High School in Omaha, Nebraska.

Clip rings?

Ban: **44 percent**
Do not ban: **56 percent**

Laura Gehrman, seventeen, pierced her own lip last year and wears her lip ring to school in Brillion, Wisconsin. It's "a form of self-expression."

AVONDALE MIDDLE SCHOOL
MEDIA CENTER

Taken from: "Teens & Freedom: 10th Annual Survey Results." www.usaweekend.com/.

and they said nothing about *plaid* sport coats. So William was following the rules—while making a statement.

It wasn't until a couple of months into the school year when I realized that William had been resisting the uniform code all along—without saying a word. He had pinned small, metal campaign-style buttons with T-shirt and CD music sayings on them all over the front of his coat. Those sayings, although not vulgar, would have gotten William or any other student in trouble—if they had been large enough to be noticed.

Acts of Quiet Defiance

Having noticed them, I quietly told William that I admired his originality, and then shared his secret with a few of his other teachers. They too appreciated his creative act of quiet defiance. We never dreamed of turning him in. You see, we all understood that despite the many benefits of uniforms, one of the main drawbacks is their suppression of individuality.

Generally, I don't like the idea of school uniforms, but I have come to see some of their benefits. I recognize that, in the classroom, uniform dress puts all my students on even footing. Even understanding those benefits, however, I still admire those creative student efforts that say, "Here I am! Look at me!"

Kids will always find ways to preserve their individual identities in spite of uniforms; the real question is whether teachers and administrators can keep up with their subversions.

Subversive Ideas Are Limitless

The variety of subversive ideas is limitless. And the dress code has become cumbersome to enforce as numerous amendments have been added to it in an effort to deal with those subversions.

Consider hair. Hair colors and styles are one outlet for students' creativity and individuality. Stuck with a uniform hair length rule, some students began to appear with gel-fortified spikes on their heads. Soon, spikes more than 3 inches in length were outlawed. Streaks of color—and whole heads of "inhuman" hair colors such as maroon, green, and orange—soon adorned students' heads. But not for long. The colors faded as the dress code rules on hair grew.

Or facial hair. This has always been a big "no-no," but some guys did start sporting a few hairs on their chins. As the goatees grew thicker, the trend was stifled by administration who made the offenders buy throw-away razors and shave at school.

What about socks and shoes? No one thought to include *those* in the code. In the winter, some kids strolled the hallways with shoes that had outlandishly high heels and thick soles. Socks . . . were multicolored and sported unusual patterns and designs. In

At Harrison Middle School in Albuquerque, teachers check the clothing of students arriving for the first day of school in 1997, when Harrison instituted a new dress code allowing only black or white clothing.

summer, backless beach shoes were worn until the code was adjusted to require leather shoes. Students soon found backless leather shoes that didn't really follow the code.

Or jewelry. Earrings were never an issue until the guys started wearing them. First, hoop earrings were banned because of safety issues. Later, to avoid being labeled sexist, the dress code was changed to allow earrings for boys. Then students started wearing multiple earrings to show their individuality. Some took to sporting several pairs of earrings on the tops or lobes of their ears. So the code was changed to allow only one earring per ear.

Too Hard to Keep Up

The bottom line is that the uniform dress code can't keep up with all the changes made as students search for their unique identities. Enforcement is a nightmare. Who has time? Clearly, teachers and administrators don't. We have already spent too much time punishing kids like William. Kids will always find new ways to express themselves, to stretch the rules. Let's just focus our energy on teaching them. Isn't that what it's all about?

FOUR

School Uniforms Are Good for Parents and Students

Cheryl Larkin

Cheryl Larkin was a longtime opponent of school uniforms until her young daughter entered a school that required them. After four years' experience with the uniforms, Larkin has become a convert. In the following selection, she details the reasons why she changed her mind. Instead of uniforms being more expensive than regular clothes, she found them to be reasonably priced. She also discovered that uniforms did not stifle individuality and that students just expressed themselves in other ways. Larkin admires the way uniforms create a safe environment and erase class differences between kids, and she likes their convenience. Larkin is a Web site designer/promoter and a mother.

I came across an article recently on AC [Associated Content] called "Should Schools Have Dress Codes," which was published on October 16, 2006, and it got me thinking about this issue as it is one that is front and center in my life.

My 8-year old daughter attends a wonderful charter school and has since she began kindergarten. When first deciding to enroll my daughter I had to weigh the pros and cons of school uniforms, which are mandatory at this particular charter school.

Before this decision I was what you would call anti-uniforms. I was one sided about this issue and sadly unwilling to entertain arguments for school uniforms. I was of the mind that uniforms stifled a child's ability to be unique and gladly show their personalities in what they wore. I believed that a child's individuality was based on what they wore. Now after 4 years of my daughter wearing a school uniform my views have changed.

Many people state that school uniforms cost more than buying regular clothes. I have found that you can get uniforms for just about the same price as regular clothes just before school starts. I buy my daughter's uniforms at Target about 2 weeks before school starts. I buy at least 3 pants, 5 shirts and either 2 dresses or pairs of skorts or a combination. This allows my daughter to still have

Sixteen-year-old Angelica Arseno tries on school uniforms at Craft Clothes in New York City.

a little control over what she wears each day all while abiding by the school uniform policy.

The beauty of this is I can wash all her school uniforms during the weekend and then I don't have to worry about whether she has clean clothes during the week at all. As far as spending more money, I find that is not true. By having the school uniforms my daughter's regular clothes last longer as they are not worn as much and I have to replace them less often, thus spending less money.

Kids Can Show Personalities in Other Ways

Even though the charter school has a school uniform policy all of the children are still unique and they all know that. They show their personalities with accessories, shoes and most importantly with words and actions. The uniforms force the children to find other appropriate ways to express themselves. Is that a bad thing? I don't think so. I love that my daughter can express herself properly with words. The school gives the children plenty of opportunities to show their personalities, like show and tell, craft projects, and even certain homework assignments.

The school also has many free dress days where the children can wear what they want. They also have theme days, where the children can wear costumes, pajamas, etc. The children all love these days and look forward to them.

Another benefit to the school uniforms is when there are class trips. My daughter's school schedules multiple class trips each year. Every child gets a special badge stating the school's name, address and phone number to wear on the class trips, which is great, but the uniforms also give a visual notice of the group the children are with. If God forbid, a child does get lost, then it is easy to describe what the child was wearing. Any form of safety for class trips is a good thing in my book.

Uniforms Are an Equalizer

Having school uniforms also eliminates the possibility of children being harassed because of their economic standing. Nearly 30 years after elementary school I still remember one girl who was

Should Public Schools Require Uniforms?

Yes. School uniforms help prevent gang violence and bullying, discrimination based on income level or style choice, formation of cliques, and distraction from learning.

81 percent (4,079 votes)

No. Students should be allowed to express themselves through their clothing and learn to respect and appreciate each others' differences.

13 percent (679 votes)

No, but there should be a strict dress code in each school that does its best to address the problems associated with clothing selection.

5 percent (255 votes)

None of the above.

1 percent (40 votes)

Taken from: "The Edutopia Poll, 2007." www.edutopia.org/.

constantly made fun of because she wore ragged clothes and never had the newest fashions. I always felt bad for her because no one bothered to find out anything about her. They simply judged her because of the clothes she wore. It turns out she had 3 siblings, her father ran off and her mother had a medical condition that kept her from working a steady job. Her mother simply didn't have the money to buy new clothes all the time. Children should not be judged because of their clothing.

Unfortunately many children today wear baggy clothes to school to hide weapons, while others wear specific clothes to advertise they are a member of a particular gang. Having school uniforms eliminates both of these issues, at least while the children are at school.

School is a child's first job. It is a place to learn and grow. It is to be taken seriously. School uniforms help the children know that they are off to work. In 1987 all 360 students at a school in Baltimore, Maryland voluntarily began wearing school uniforms. Nine years later the school principal reported that attendance was up, suspensions were down, children were more focused on schoolwork, fights were less frequent, and test scores were going up. In 1994 California's Long Beach Unified School District adopted a mandatory school uniform policy and records indicate that since then school crime has dropped by 76 percent and attendance is at an all time high.

While no formal testing has been done I believe that as long as both the parents and the school work together to allow creativity and personality to show through on the children then there is nothing wrong with school uniforms.

I really did struggle with the decision to put my daughter in a school that required school uniforms but in the end I decided the benefits of the school were well worth my daughter having to wear a uniform. After 4 years of attending the school I am now glad that I made the decision and truly believe that school uniforms are actually a good thing.

FIVE

School Uniforms Eliminate Fashion Competition

Taylor Armerding

As the local town of Lawrence, Massachusetts, considers adopting a school uniform policy, Taylor Armerding, a self-professed "aging hippie," aligns himself with the pro-uniform faction despite his anti-uniform past. He writes that uniforms offer "a relatively simple way to eliminate a meaningless, but very expensive, competition"—that is, the competition to keep up with the latest fashions. Instead of competing over who has the best clothes, he argues, students would be better served competing in more substantial areas like sports, academics, or drama. Armerding is the associate editorial page editor of the North Andover, Massachusetts, *Eagle-Tribune*.

Go for it, Lawrence [Massachusetts town considering uniforms]. Bring on school uniforms.

Yeah, I know—rank hypocrisy, coming from an aging hippie who slouched around his college campus in moccasins, jeans and a pea coat about 35 years ago. But hey, politicians change their minds all the time. When they do, they say it's because their thinking has "evolved." And I consider myself a much higher—if older—life form than I was back then.

Besides, this evolution isn't political. I'm not trolling for votes. I've come to this view through the purest of motives—my passionate advocacy "for the children." Did you know children are our future?

This is also a chance for Lawrence to be a leader. Its schools don't lead the state in anything worth talking about at the moment, but I think it could be showing the rest of you unenlightened systems the way on this. If all goes as expected, the School Committee will vote this week to require uniforms in the fall for students at the new, $110 million high school.

School officials pitch it as a way to make the campus of the mammoth new school safer. With uniforms, it will be easier to identify anybody who doesn't belong there.

Maybe, although it seems that if the clothes are being sold at local businesses, anybody who wants to sneak into the school can just go buy them.

Fashion and Social Pressure

Questions Worth Discussing

- Is there too much pressure to wear fashionable clothes in your school system?

- Do you plan what you are going to wear for school?

- Do pupils laugh if you dress differently?

- What would you say to them if this happened to you?

Taken from: Claire Lovey, "Forced to Wear a Skirt." www.britishcouncil.org/.

Better Reasons for Uniforms

But there are other, better reasons for students—even public school students—to wear uniforms.

For the past couple of decades, school administrators who think it's a fine idea to put just about every kid in the school on the honor roll, have been harping on "cooperation over competition." Everybody can win, they say, if we just get rid of this concept of winners and losers.

That isn't the way the real world works, of course, in everything from athletics to science to the law. And even the most "progressive" school leaders don't really believe this. Otherwise, they'd ban keeping score in interscholastic sports. But one area where competition in school is demonstrably corrosive and ought to be eliminated is in clothes. Kids, or more likely their parents, waste a colossal amount of time, energy and money trying to keep up with whatever changing fashions are popular at school. Uniforms are a relatively simple way to eliminate a meaningless, but very expensive, competition.

I'm sure there will be at least a few screams of protest that this will crush the individual expression of the students—that it will force them all to become automatons. That this may even violate the First Amendment.

Kids Are Already Wearing Uniforms

Anybody who takes a walk through just about any school knows this is rubbish. You will see that, with minor variations, the kids are already wearing uniforms. It's just that these uniforms are dictated by competing peer groups instead of school administrators. Kids all wear pretty much the same thing because they don't want to be individuals. They want to fit in.

It has been this way for generations. In the '50s, the guys all rolled their cigarette packs into the sleeve of their T-shirts and slicked their hair back in a ducktail like the teen idols of the era. In the '60s, everybody tried to look like the Beatles. Today, hip-hop rules and the pants sit about 6 inches south of the waistline and the sneakers cost $100 or more.

Students in Basel, Switzerland, model a uniform created by Swiss designer Tanja Klein. The uniforms are an experiment aimed at leveling out differences among students.

Sure, fashion can be creative. But clothes are about the worst possible way to express true individuality. An expensive, cutting-edge outfit doesn't have anything to do with how well a student does on a test, in a game or on a project. Neither does a random ensemble pulled off the Salvation Army rack. If a kid is a great athlete, how stylish the clothes he or she wears at school doesn't change that.

If schools were insisting that everybody had to study one subject only, like science, then the complaints about destroying individuality would have some merit. But uniforms offer the chance for students to celebrate their individuality in the areas that matter—science, sports, drama, math, literature, law, politics, the trades or any other possible career path. Get rid of the clothes competition and free the kids to concentrate on their individual interests and aptitudes. That's supposed to be the goal of education anyway.

For generations, good teachers, mentors and parents have told kids that looks and clothes don't really matter—it is what's inside that counts. School uniforms are one good way to give that message some meaning.

SIX

Dress Codes Allow Parents and Teachers to Avoid Real Issues

Chris Bailey

> In the following selection Chris Bailey writes of her delight at the news of a local Illinois school district's elimination of a ten-year-old dress code after complaints from students, faculty, and parents. As a student, Bailey led her own fight against a school policy requiring girls at her Minnesota school to wear dresses, even on cold winter days. As an adult, she found more reasons to dislike dress codes. She argues that dress codes stifle individuality, create a follow-the-pack mentality, and are a way to cover up problems without getting to the real cause. Bailey is an editorial columnist for the *Daily Herald*, a newspaper in Arlington Heights, Illinois.

My mother thought I was an anarchist, she being one of those who looked forward to Easter week for the frilly dresses and floppy hats that could be acquired without accompanying guilt.

Her daughter, on the other hand, led the destruction of the school dress code from her seat on the student council—a code that then required girls to wear dresses to school. Every day. No exceptions, even for a –30 degree Minnesota winter day. I'm not sure my mother ever forgave her inveterate tomboy

[for] what she believed was heresy, but neither of us ever changed our minds.

Which is why I took great delight when the powers that be at Carpentersville Middle School [CMS] and Community Unit School District 300 last week [in July 2006] eradicated a 10-year-old dress code that had limited middle school kids to khaki, white and blue clothing. The decision had followed complaints from kids, faculty and parents.

Score one for individualism. Score one for a lower family clothing budget. Score one for officials finally admitting the dress code did more to lower self-esteem than raise it, the erstwhile excuse for regimenting into bland automatons kids standing at the very cusp of The Age of Self-Identification. Rather than teaching them that how they dress and act identifies them for both good and ill, dress codes do the opposite, teaching them to hide behind sameness. They mandate the very same follow-the-pack mentality that officials and parents try to subvert just two years later when kids get to high school and the pack is more likely to be doing drugs, drinking and having sex. No wonder kids are confused.

Dress Codes Just an Attempt to Cover Up Problems

When dress codes are implemented, discipline and behavior are usually problems. As if the shoes were starting the fights, the jeans were issuing the insults or the shirts were smoking on the sly in the bathroom. But it's far easier for the adults to just order up a new look than to actually address the problems, you know, by determining who is breaking the rules and causing the problems and doing something about it.

Dress codes are always considered great equalizers, too; attempts to blind kids to the reality that there are rich and poor, fashion fanatics and fashion frumps, and those who put great store on surface trappings while others care more what's inside. Rather than accept and teach to those realities, though, we attempt to cover them up with khaki, plaid, knit golf shirts and ties.

What the CMS dress code did was ostracize its students, mostly poor and minority, among other District 300 students. They were the only ones, apparently, in a need of such a rigid dress code. And true to reality, they were harassed by other district students because of it. Not exactly the result officials and other adults had sought, but nonetheless predictable.

And we can't forget the parents, either, since they are the genesis of many a dress code request. Far easier, it seems, to push for a dress code than to simply tell a child that $79 jeans and fashion

Celebrating the last day of school in 1997, students wear baggy clothing outside a movie theater in Albuquerque. Several styles of these pants would be forbidden in many school districts because they hang so far below the waist.

The Dress Code at One California High School

Scotts Valley High School does not permit the following while attending classes:

Bare feet

Excessively short shorts or skirts

Exposure of undergarments

Exposure of rear

Clothing that exposes midriff, stomach, or lower abdomen

Revealing or low-cut tops of any kind

Strapless or backless tops

Clothing that insults any person on the basis of race, religion, gender, sexual orientation, disability, or appearance (CA Ed. Code A8537)

Clothing or accessories that advertise alcohol or tobacco (including accessories on backpacks or binders)

Clothing that promotes violence or drug use

Accessories that pose a physical threat to students or staff

Gang-related clothing (CA Ed. Code 35183, 35294.1.1)

Clothing that distracts or disrupts the normal function of the school or classroom

Taken from: *Santa Cruz Sentinel*, June 8, 2007.

make-up are out of the question budget-wise, not to mention ludicrous for a 10-year-old. Far easier, it seems, to push for a dress code than to teach a child that self-esteem comes from effort and accomplishment, sometimes even from overcoming failure or circumstances, not from something anyone can buy at the store.

Dress codes have always been more to make life comfortable for adults who like things to stay a certain way than to provide any real benefit to those whose lives are regimented by them. That hasn't really changed much in 35 years. Nor have the complaints by the kids, some of whom still apparently feel compelled to rebel against the regimentation.

Thank heaven for that. We old-time boat rockers are getting a little long in the tooth. We could use some new wave-makers added to the ranks. No dress code required, of course.

SEVEN

Uniforms Create a Better Learning Environment

Matt Wennersten

In the following viewpoint teacher Matt Wennersten writes about his school's new uniform policy. Wennersten argues that the policy helps teach students that it is appropriate to wear professional clothes in a work environment. Many of Wennersten's students were not aware that job interviews require a uniform of sorts, and he notes that wearing uniforms at school helps teach his kids "the rules of the game." The new policy also reduces time students used to spend in his class comparing and fighting over clothing. "When my students enter the classroom in uniform, half of my classroom management is done—I have a group of professionals, ready to work," he writes. Wennersten teaches math at Bell Multicultural High School in Columbia Heights, Washington, D.C.

My school recently introduced uniforms: collared blue or white shirt and khaki pants. There has been a lot of support from parents, and a lot of dissent from students. The school has worked hard to convince students to wear the uniform: assemblies, letters and phone calls home, and, two weeks ago, kids being asked to go home and change if they come to school out of uniform.

Matt Wennersten, "Uniform Fuss Misses Big Picture," *Common Denominator*, February 6, 2006. www.thecommondenominator.com. Copyright © 2006 The Common Denominator. Reproduced by permission.

To the school, it's about safety, pride and discipline. Random kids from off the street stick out when everyone is in uniform. Gang colors vanish. Distractions like expensive clothing or plunging cleavage are minimized. Wearing a uniform means you're part of a team; there's a sense of belonging and community. Plus, once you have a few pairs of khakis, it's cheap and easy getting ready for school. These are the positives.

A friend of mine recently commented that "it's troubling that public schools that have uniforms are predominantly minority

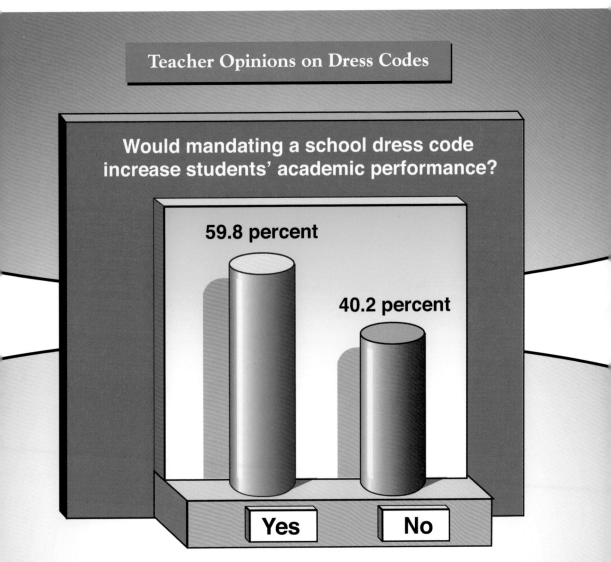

Teacher Opinions on Dress Codes

Would mandating a school dress code increase students' academic performance?

59.8 percent

40.2 percent

Yes

No

Taken from: www.teach-nology.com/. July 10, 2007.

and poor." Are we preparing our students for a life in uniform, i.e. the military, low-end service jobs or prison? Are we requiring uniforms simply to keep order, like (the book) *1984* writ small?

On the flip side, why do expensive private schools have uniforms? Are we helping our kids learn the rules of the game, where image is part of opportunity? Many of my students don't know that there is a uniform for job interviews: coat and tie, conservative skirt and blouse. Last summer, a Bell student had an internship at the World Bank. He noticed that when he dressed professionally, he was treated like an adult. He liked it so much that he was noticeably snappier when this school year began, even before the uniform policy.

That student is the exception. Repeatedly, I hear from the kids: "How can you ask us to be independent thinkers when you don't allow us to express our individuality?" And they have a point: part of wearing a uniform is about conformity and following the rules. Historically, many of the rules were there to keep people like my students out of power. On one hand, we encourage our students to speak out against injustice and to act for social change, yet on the other hand, we impose conditions on their life that they perceive as unjust. I doubt the school would win in court if we were to suspend a student for not wearing a uniform, and rightly so; in America, we have a right to a free and fair education.

Setting a Good Example for the Students

Even so, I strongly support uniforms for students. Before uniforms, I wore a tie almost every day. Since the introduction of the uniform, I've worn the uniform every day. I do this to support the administration in encouraging kids to wear it. I do it to support the kids, by showing that it's OK to wear a pair of khakis and a button down in a professional work environment. I also do it because it helps me approach the workplace in the right frame of mind. If I'm wearing a tie, I act differently than if I'm wearing a tie-dye T-shirt. And I support the uniform because I think that it promotes better education among our students.

I believe that the fuss about uniforms among the kids is missing a bigger picture. It's not about individuality. It's about better learning. There are many ways to express your individuality besides clothing; it's a sign of how inarticulate my students can be that they fear losing this one outlet from 8:30 to 3:30. I don't condemn that—I like fashion and I respect the fact that our kids want to show some style. Yet, I've seen as a teacher that the style has come at the expense of learning.

Some feel that if students are not focusing so much on clothes, they will pay more attention in class.

Uniforms Make Kids Ready to Work

Somewhere along the way, my kids have internalized the message that the way you look is more important than who you are, that your worth is measured by bling on the outside, not knowledge on the inside. The uniform has been a great leveler. The kids know who "has it" and who "wants it" intellectually, and now there's no gang color or cool outfit to hide behind. If you want to stand out, you have to do it academically, and the group you belong to is the school group. When my students enter the classroom in uniform, half of my classroom management is done—I have a group of professionals, ready to work. Contrast this with the "before" case: I have vivid memories of 10-minute student conversations like "Is that a North Face jacket? That big yellow one? He looks like Big Bird!" This leads to fights.

I don't believe that our kids should be put on an assembly line and force-fed certain ideas. I believe very strongly that the strength of our country has been innovation and original thinking. I see the uniform as helping this. My kids rail against the uniform, in part because they have no other realm in which to express themselves. My job is to give them the keys, the essential knowledge and skills required to be a poet, an astronomer, a hacker, a moviemaker, a business owner. My second-grade teacher used to ask me to "put on my thinking cap" when confronted with a tough problem. So now I tell my students: "Put on your uniform."

EIGHT

Teachers Should Have a Dress Code

Charles Waggoner

> In the following viewpoint Charles Waggoner writes that since students have dress codes, it is appropriate that teachers should have a dress code, too. In his opinion teachers and other school staff who dress professionally convey a high regard for education. "We need for our students and community to see teachers as professional and not as their pals, dressing alike in jeans and t-shirts," he writes. Waggoner is superintendent of the Havana Community United School District in Havana, Illinois.

To paraphrase Leo Tolstoy, "Happy school districts are all alike; every unhappy district is unhappy in its own way."

The district where I am superintendent became unhappy in its own unique way in April 2000 when newly elected board members suggested that a few teachers were not dressing in a professional manner and needed to wear more appropriate attire. This seemed like an innocuous request on the part of the board at the time. All they were asking was that teachers refrain from wearing blue denim jeans on "casual day" (payday Friday), which had become the unofficial custom in our district.

The board pointed to mandatory dress guidelines for Hamburger University at McDonald's corporate training site in Oak Brook,

Charles Waggoner, "Blue Denim Blues," *School Administrator*, February 2002. www.aasa.org. Reproduced by permission.

Ill., and for the professional staff at Disneyland, both of which stipulate that business casual does not include jeans of any type. Wouldn't it also help to reinforce teachers as role models if they returned to a more professional look? Can't schools set their dress standards for staff as high as McDonald's or Disney?

A Sample Case

For decades, students have been scrutinized by school officials who could send them home for inappropriate clothing. Almost every school, with few exceptions, has a student dress code, but few districts in Illinois have any dress code statements pertaining to teachers.

When the "no-jeans policy" was distributed to the teachers following the board's action, it took only a few days before a grievance was threatened, charging that the district had failed to discuss changes in the contract with "respect to wages, hours and other terms and conditions of employment."

The advice of the school district's counsel was to rescind the dress code directive and move on. A teacher's dress code policy was in his legal opinion "a very slippery slope" that was not worth the pain involved nor the time it would take to get a decision on the issue. His advice was taken and the board and administration collectively blinked and rescinded the dress code edict.

The no-denim-jeans matter—some would say fiasco—resulted in "Casual Friday" becoming the norm most days of the week for a certain group of teachers who were determined to demonstrate to the board and administration just what they thought of tampering with their grooming standards. The majority of the staff refrained from wearing blue jeans, either out of respect to administrative wishes or a personal sense of professionalism.

No Specific Precedent Set

In researching the legal aspects of a teacher dress code, I found that historically the courts have upheld the school administration when the application of teacher dress was reasonable and intended to serve a legitimate purpose. Some dress code decisions

Karen Moxley from Texas participates in a discussion about dress codes for teachers during a National Education Association conference in 2005.

have favored boards and some have gone in favor of the teachers. The unique circumstances in each case make it impossible to establish any trends or judicial tendencies.

The cases give some direction regarding what the courts may approve and what they may not. Blue jeans are something a person can put on and take off, unlike facial hair, which is part of the projection of a person 24 hours a day. Teachers are free to "be themselves" in blue jeans on weekends and before and after school hours so the courts have stated that a rule against blue jeans is clearly not a First Amendment violation.

A Sampling of Teacher Dress Codes in Texas

School District	Staff Dress Code?	Guidelines
Allen, DeSoto, Garland, Highland Park	No	Principals determine what is appropriate for each campus; certain attire is allowed on special days
Arlington, Carroll, Carrollton-Farmers Branch, Coppell, Frisco, Lewisville, Plano	Yes	Dress is to be clean, neat, and in a manner appropriate for assignments or as otherwise established by the site
Cedar Hill	Yes	No blue jeans, tennis shoes, or printed or casual T-shirts
Dallas	Yes	Project a professional image for the employee, school, and district; men must wear ties; womens slacks or skirts no shorter than 2 inches above the knee; jeans, shorts, revealing/provocative shirts, and flip-flops prohibited
Duncanville	Yes	Styles of clothing should be modest and tasteful; women are encouraged to wear hose, men shall tuck in their shirts
Grand Prairie	Yes	Unacceptable at all times: short shorts; bare midriffs/strapless tops; stretch garments; disruptive makeup, hairstyles, or tattoos/body art; caps, hats, and visors; visible tongue and body piercing, except for ears
Grapevine-Colleyville	Yes	Teachers should dress appropriately
Irving	Yes	Assumes the wearing of basic foundation garments and appropriate skirt/short length; men are expected to wear shirt and tie
Lancaster	Yes	Males must wear dress shirts, slacks, and ties; women must wear dresses and skirts that are no shorter than 2 inches above the knee or dress slacks and hose
Richardson	Yes	Standards set by principals and other supervisors; repeated violations will result in discipline up to and including termination
Rockwall	Yes	Staff members may not wear clothing prohibited by the student dress code; male staff may have facial hair that is well groomed
Wylie	Yes	Calls for employees to be neatly groomed and dressed in a way that conforms to local etiquette and decorum

Taken from: "District on Teacher Dress: Have Some Class," *Dallas Morning News,* September 15, 2006.

Dress Codes Convey Professional Image

A school dress code must be related reasonably to a legitimate educational purpose, which must be justified. For many students the classroom teacher is the most professional person they see in the course of a day. We need for our students and community to see teachers as professionals and not as their pals, dressing alike in jeans and t-shirts. Some recent evidence turned up by Katie Swanger, dean of faculty at Heald College's School of Business and Technology, indicates that students may judge the performance of teachers higher if they are dressed professionally.

The California School Boards Association has an optional policy for local boards to adopt. It states: "The governing board believes that since teachers serve as role models, they should maintain professional standards of dress and grooming. Just as overall attitude and instructional competency contribute to a productive learning environment, so do appropriate dress and grooming. The board encourages staff during school hours to wear clothing that demonstrates their high regard for education and presents an image consistent with their job responsibilities. Clothes that may be appropriate for shop instructors or gym teachers may not be appropriate for classroom teachers."

The administration should set an appropriate professional standard for the staff in their own professional dress and require the same for the teachers. Ask yourself this question: Have you ever interviewed a teaching candidate who was wearing blue jeans and tennis shoes?

Would anyone go to an educational interview—or any job interview—looking less than his or her best? I think not. Why then should teachers settle for less in their day-to-day teaching appearance?

NINE

Research Does Not Prove Dress Codes Are Effective

Debra Viadero

In the following essay Debra Viadero points to the dichoto-my between how effective schools think uniform policies are and the research showing just the opposite. She cites David Brunsma's oft-cited study showing that uniform poli-cies do not work in the way that administrators believe. According to the study, uniforms do not curb violence or behavioral problems, and they do not increase academic achievement. Despite this, teachers, administrators, and parents repeatedly note improvement after uniform poli-cies are adopted. Viadero is associate editor for *Education Week* and specializes in educational research.

There's something about a student in uniform, muses Principal Rudolph Saunders as he scans the busy lunchroom here at Stephen Decatur Middle School. Under Decatur's policy, all stu-dents wear the standard school attire consisting of khaki pants with polo shirts in white, burgundy, or navy blue. Some of the shirts also sport an embroidered Decatur eagle, an optional embellishment.

Saunders' instincts tell him that students behave better when they're dressed alike, that they fight less and focus on their schoolwork more. Plus, the uniform puts all students on a more equal social footing, regardless of whether they come from comfortable middle-class house-

Debra Viadero, "Uniform Effects?" *Education Week*, January 12, 2005. www.edweek.org. Reproduced by permission.

holds or one of the group foster-care homes that lie in Decatur's attendance zone.

"It's like night and day," Saunders says. "We have 'dress down' days, and the kids' behavior is just completely different on those days." Yet national studies on the effectiveness of school uniform policies tell a story distinctly different from educators' experiences here at Decatur, according to David L. Brunsma, a researcher at the University of Missouri–Columbia. Brunsma, an assistant professor of sociology, has been studying the movement for public school uniforms since 1996. That was the year that President [Bill] Clinton propelled the movement into the national consciousness by endorsing the idea in his State of the Union Address. In a book published in November [2005] by ScarecrowEducation, Brunsma seeks to set the record straight on what uniforms can and cannot do for public schools.

And his general conclusion is "not much."

Uniforms Do Not Solve Problems

"Despite the media coverage," Brunsma writes in *The School Uniform Movement and What It Tells Us About American Education*, "despite the anecdotal meanderings of politicians, community members, educators, board members, parents, and students, uniforms have not been effective at attacking the very outcomes and issues they were assumed to aid."

That means, he says, that uniform policies don't curb violence or behavioral problems in schools. They don't cultivate student self-esteem and motivation. They don't balance the social-status differences that often separate students. And they don't improve academic achievement. (In fact, uniforms may even be associated with a small detrimental effect on achievement in reading, his research shows.)

Brunsma's message is not new. With research partner Kerry Rockquemore, he arrived at similar conclusions in a 1998 study published in the peer-reviewed *Journal of Educational Research*. Among the first of its kind, the study was just a drop of evidence in an area of study that was thirsting for some solid signs of effectiveness.

"We were actually a little bit shocked that [uniforms] didn't have the kind of impact people were discussing," Brunsma says of his early research with Rockquemore. He says the two cooked up the idea for the study one day over coffee after they had read a national newspaper headline pointing to Clinton's mention of school uniforms as a possible cure for schools' ills. "The idea of school uniforms does seem commonsensical as a way to equalize social status," he adds.

Brunsma has expanded his work since then and compiled it all in his book, which is probably the most exhaustive collection to date of quantitative research on the nationwide movement to embrace school uniforms.

He bases his own conclusions on analyses of two massive databases. They are the National Educational Longitudinal Study of 1988, a federal data archive that tracks a nationally representative sample of 8th graders throughout their years of schooling, and the Early Childhood Longitudinal Study, a more recent database that began tracking children from preschool on in 1998.

In conducting hundreds of analyses, Brunsma looks for effects among individual students and entire schools, and among younger children and teenagers. He also controls for differences that might also account for varying test scores, such as the socioeconomic status or race of students. And, for the most part, he continues to come up empty-handed on any evidence that school uniform policies are effective.

Real-Life Conclusions Are Different

Yet such conclusions run counter to the real-life experiences of some of the districts that have been at the forefront of the school-uniform movement. Take the Long Beach Unified School District in California. In 1994, the 97,200-student urban district, located in the southern part of the state, became the first public school district in the nation to require all students in grades K-8 to wear uniforms. A two-year evaluation of that effort, conducted from 1993 to 1995, turned up some

Research on the Effects of School Uniforms

Outcome	Kindergarten	K–1st Changes	8th Grade	10th Grade
Climate				
Students' perceptions of safety climate	NS	NS	NS	n/a
Principals' perceptions of safety climate	NS	n/a	**	n/a
Students' perceptions of education climate	n/a	NS	NS	n/a
Principals' perceptions of education climate	n/a	n/a	NS	n/a
Parental involvement	n/a	NS	n/a	n/a
Achievement				
Composite test	n/a	n/a	NS	**
Reading/literacy	NS	NS	NS	**
Math	NS	NS	NS	NS
Science	n/a	n/a	NS	NS
History	n/a	n/a	NS	NS
General knowledge	NS	NS	n/a	n/a
Attendance	n/a	n/a	NS	NS

NS = The effect is not statistically significant.
n/a = Data or outcomes are not available.
** = There is a negative significant effect.

Taken from: David L. Brunsma, "School Uniform Policies in Public Schools," *Principal*, January/February 2006.

remarkable improvements: a 28 percent drop in suspension rates at the elementary level, a 36 percent decline in middle school suspensions, a 51 percent decrease in fights in grades K-8, and a 34 percent drop in assault and battery in elementary and middle schools.

An employee stocks the school uniform racks at La Ideal Baby Store in Doral, Florida. Many school officials think that wearing uniforms improves student conduct.

To Brunsma's way of thinking, though, that study suffered from two major problems. For starters, it involved just one district and, second, it failed to account for other changes, such as demographic shifts, that might also explain the results. Brunsma says newer case studies looking at uniform-adoption efforts in schools in Baltimore, Denver, and Aldine, Texas, a suburban Houston district—all of which also point to positive effects—have an additional shortcoming. Besides being largely anecdotal, they were sponsored by French Toast, a leading manufacturer of school uniforms based in Martinsville, Va.

"If you look at the published stuff on this, the ones that conclude positive results, by and large come from clothiers," he says, noting that school uniforms have grown into a multimillion-dollar industry. Another study of school uniforms was financed by Dodgeville, Wis.–based Lands' End Inc., which started its school uniform division in 1997.

The statistics seem to matter little, however, to parents and school leaders here in Prince George's County, Md., a middle-class, largely African-American suburb bordering Washington [D.C.] that includes Stephen Decatur Middle School, or to the thousands of other public schools around the country that continue to embrace the use of uniforms.

In fact, Brunsma estimates that as many as 27 percent of all public elementary schools by the year 2000 had some sort of uniform policy in place. Those schools tend to be in areas where families are disadvantaged, or in places like Prince George's County where most students are members of minority groups.

The impetus for uniforms in the 135,000-student Prince George's County district came in the mid-1990s from a vocal group of parents. By the start of this school year [2004–2005], 80 of the district's 196 schools had adopted either mandatory or voluntary uniform policies. The first county high school to join that list adopted a school uniform policy this year.

"When a school or a PTA decides to go in that direction, they go in that direction," says Howard A. Burnett, the district's chief administrator for human resources. For the most part, he says, the district has neither encouraged schools to adopt the practice nor discouraged them, choosing instead to let local communities take the lead and to support their efforts.

For that reason, Prince George's officials never formally tracked the impact that uniform policies have had in their schools. Neither has Decatur, which began requiring uniforms in 1998.

Test Scores Going Up

But Betty Mikesell-Bailey, the school-improvement resource teacher at Decatur, says test scores have been going up and in-school suspensions have been going down ever since the middle school made the switch. Once targeted for "reconstitution" because of its low scores under the state's former testing program, Decatur has been improving every year. Now it meets most of its achievement targets on Maryland's new assessment. The lone exception comes among special education students, who still fail as a group to make the annual test-score gains state officials expect.

Whether those improvements have anything to do with uniforms, Mikesell-Bailey can't say for sure. She's fairly certain, though, that the policy has cut down on the teasing to which middle school children subject one another.

"Children at this age are always going to find something wrong with someone," says Mikesell-Bailey. She tells a story about some boys she observed watching a fellow student make a presentation in the school's media center. She noticed the boys were making fun of the other boy's sneakers, which were plain white, in contrast to their more fashionable two-tone shoes. It was the only clothing item that differentiated the student from his classmates, because there is some leeway in the type of shoes students can wear.

"What I'm saying is," Mikesell-Bailey adds, "children at this age are so impressed with dress that, if we can eliminate that little aspect of their daily lives and get their minds focused on academics, that's half the battle."

On that point, even the students agree. Without clothing to focus on, they say, students pick on one another for other reasons.

None of this is to say, of course, that these students like their uniforms. Seventh grader Aaron Morton, for one, says "uniforms are uncomfortable. They make you feel all stiff like robots or something." Other students have similar complaints. "People can't be who they are if they have to wear the same thing every day," says Alexis Richardson, who's also in 7th grade.

Uniforms Have a History of Dehumanizing the Lower Class

To some degree, Brunsma believes the students may have a point when it comes to the potentially dehumanizing effects of uniforms. Some of his historical research suggests, for example, that school uniforms originated in England in the 16th century as a way to signal the lower-class status of some children.

"Most people assume uniforms are heavily correlated with elite status, but early on, they were used as a marker for orphans and charity children," he says. That's why he's worried now that most of the public schools that have adopted uniform policies serve student populations that are often disadvantaged.

While he can't prove that uniforms are purposely being used to stigmatize groups of students, he does marshal some statistical evidence to suggest that they don't help when it comes to bolstering self-esteem in the early grades. One of uniform proponents' hopes has been that, by evening out social status differences between students, uniforms could raise the sense of self-worth of students from poor families.

But educators and parents in Prince George's County also note that uniform policies may carry benefits that studies like Brunsma's do not measure. For example, J. Showell, the middle school's security officer, says the uniform policy makes it easier for him to spot outsiders coming into the building. "I can scan a whole group of folks and see those people that belong to Decatur," he says.

Mikesell-Bailey, Decatur's school-improvement resource teacher, says the uniforms also flag students when they try to ditch class and head home. She occasionally sees them along the road as she drives to pick up lunch at a nearby shopping center. "When I see the uniform, I always stop, because I know it's one of my children," she says.

Parents Like Them

Rhonda E. Chandler, the parent of a 7th grader at Decatur, likes not having to buy more expensive designer clothes or worrying that her child will change into less appropriate clothing in the school restroom or on the bus going to school. "I love the fact that my daughter wears a uniform," says Chandler, who also is

Students at San Antonio's Mark Twain Middle School mill around campus in their uniforms.

president of the school's PTA. "It's just one less thing to worry about."

Decatur and district officials say parental support may be the biggest reason for the policy's longevity here. Elsewhere around the country, in comparison, some schools and districts have abandoned efforts to impose uniform requirements on students.

A case in point is Highland-Goffe's Falls Elementary School in New Hampshire, where Principal James Paul says less-than-unanimous support from parents helped undo a short-lived experiment with mandatory uniforms in 2000–01. "We had seven very negative parents out of 454 families," says Paul. "Those seven children never wore uniforms, which, from my point of view, kind of derailed us."

After the school board declined to allow Paul to transfer those students to a different elementary school, the school scrapped the policy—even though officials said instances of bullying had decreased in the year that uniforms were worn. "I would say it was a successful failure," Paul says now.

Enforcing the Policy

To avoid a similar fate at Maryland's Decatur Middle School, educators work hard to enforce their policy. When students come to school missing regulation wear, Saunders makes a call to their parents. Repeat offenders must serve an in-school suspension. Some teachers also keep uniform items on hand for students who are new to the school.

"If a child walks in today and enrolls, in the next hour or so, I would bet you're going to see a uniform on that child," says Mikesell-Bailey. "It's because we don't want other students to see a child without a uniform."

Though enforcing the policy takes up Principal Saunders' time, it's more clear-cut and less time-consuming than trying to decide whether students are complying with the district's standard dress code. How low-cut can a girl's shirt be before it crosses from appropriate to inappropriate, for instance? How baggy is baggy?

"I would spend 60 to 90 minutes a day on dress-code violations before," says Saunders, who served as an administrator at county secondary schools with no uniform requirements before coming to Decatur. "I wouldn't be surprised if every school in the county moves to uniforms."

Still, even he concedes that uniforms alone can't overcome all the challenges that public schools face. "I think some people think if you change the clothes, everything else is going to change magically," he says. "But it all has to be part of a package."

TEN

Uniforms Are a Way of Controlling Children

Jordan Riak

In the following viewpoint Jordan Riak describes his American family's experience with the school uniform policy in Australia. After initially being charmed by the "smart" look of the uniforms, he came to a darker conclusion—that uniforms are a way of controlling children. "There is a universal belief among parents that by controlling their children's lives down to the smaller details, they can help determine their destiny, or at least steer them past the worst pitfalls," he writes. To further his argument, he cites the most common pro-uniform arguments and offers counter-arguments to them. Riak is a founder of Parents and Teachers Against Violence in Education.

As the students of Sydney Grammar paraded onto the field, a mother standing next to me gushed: "Ah! Don't they look splendid!" All were smartly uniformed of course—these sparkling university-bound professionals-to-be, future leaders of government and captains of industry. All were white. All were male.

My first impulse upon seeing my sons smartly outfitted in their first school uniforms was to photograph them and send the picture home to New Jersey for their grandparents' pride and pleasure. We were new arrivals in Australia where uniforms for schoolchildren were, and I suppose still are, standard.

Jordan Riak, "School Uniforms: Seeing Schoolchildren as Canned Sardines," *Project NoSpank*, August 16, 2002. www.nospank.net. Reproduced by permission.

But the novelty and the charm of it quickly faded.

On one occasion, my eldest son, then in his teens, was challenged and threatened by a teacher because of the trinket he was wearing on the chain around his neck. "What's this? You know jewelry is against the rules here. Get rid of it. If I see that thing again, you know what you'll be getting."

On another occasion, my middle son was ridiculed in front of his class because of a violation of the dress code. His teacher, referring to his shoes, announced: "We don't need grubs in this school." That morning, I had suggested he wear his sneakers because his school shoes were still wet from the previous day's rain.

I don't remember if my youngest son ever experienced a problem regarding the uniform. What was happening to him at that time overshadowed other concerns. He was receiving the standard treatment for dyslexia: a daily regimen of public humiliation.

There is a universal belief among parents that by controlling their children's lives down to the smaller details, they can help determine their destiny, or at least steer them past the worst pitfalls. In these rapidly changing times, the illusion is comforting, and frightened parents are apt to seize upon any strategy, including look-alike packaging of their offspring, that seems to assure their safety and success.

Uniforms Are a Way for Parents to Control Their Children

Perhaps a more accurate, though less flattering, interpretation of parents' compulsion to micromanage their children, is that they are acting, not out of a desire to protect and nurture, but rather out of their own morbid fear of freedom derived from their own overcontrolled upbringing. Such parents' first impulse is to thwart the natural freedom-striving of their children. They respond with punishments such as rigid feeding schedules for their infants, then spankings, uniforms, curfews, etc. When warmth and encouragement are most needed, they apply strictures and ice—anything to immobilize, stymie growth and forestall emancipation. The prospect that any child should have a more joyful start in life than

A teacher guides a uniformed student off the bus at St. Andrew the Apostle Elementary School in New Orleans.

they had drives them up the wall. "You can't just let kids run wild," they fume.

Having experienced two cultures, one where school uniforms are ubiquitous and the other where their use is limited mainly to Catholic schools and military academies, I now believe that school uniforms are educationally counterproductive and that the usual reasons given in support of their use are folkloric and contrary to the evidence. I believe that the regimentation of children's dress is a vestige of the sumptuary laws of the middle ages. Today, anyone attempting to promote a return to that standard for adults would be considered crazy.

The real but unspoken reason for school uniforms is that they establish in the child's mind a constant reminder, as well as create a visible symbol recognizable to everyone, of his or her inferior status. Additionally, the use of school uniforms provides the least competent teachers—the ones who constantly need to shore up their own fragile status—a ready-made excuse for asserting their authority and inflicting punishments. By these means, they create the illusion that they are engaged in useful work. Schools that require uniforms typically waste much valuable time on inspections and imposition of punishments for dress-code infractions. During my stay in New South Wales, prior to the abolition of the cane there, I found that one of the most common justifications for beating students was their being out of uniform. Schools that abandon uniforms usually show an immediate boost in student morale and a lessening of tension between students and authority figures.

The Pro-Uniform Arguments

The reasons most frequently given for the use of school uniforms are:

1) They reduce fashion-related competition between students thus freeing them to focus their attention on their studies.

2) They eliminate or reduce resentments between students of higher and lower socioeconomic classes by making them appear equal.

3) They eliminate or reduce gang-related violence by denying students the opportunity to display tribal colors.

4) They are economical because the well-made garments last for years, can be used in turn by younger siblings and are not subject to obsolescence due to changing fads.

Principals on Uniforms

Percentage of principals with school uniform policies who cite improvements in these areas:

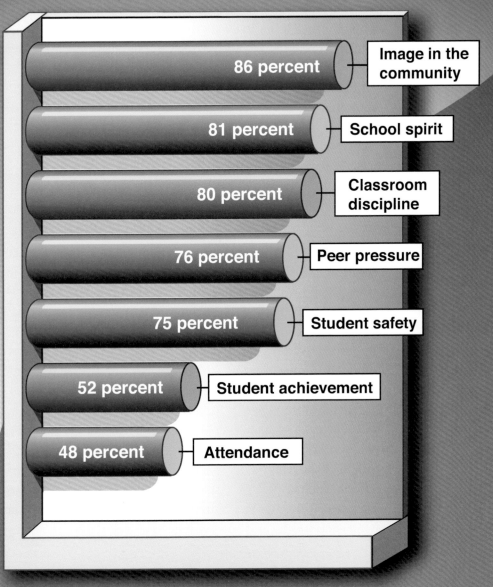

86 percent — Image in the community

81 percent — School spirit

80 percent — Classroom discipline

76 percent — Peer pressure

75 percent — Student safety

52 percent — Student achievement

48 percent — Attendance

This chart is based on a survey of a regionally diverse sample of 958 principals in California, Florida, Georgia, Illinois, Michigan, New York, Ohio, Texas, Virginia, and Washington.

Taken from: "Schools Suit Up," *American School Board Journal.* www.asbj.com/.

Now let's take a closer look. Taken in order, I contend that:

1) Fashion-related competition among youth derives from fashion-related competition among the adults who provide the model for that behavior. While children temporarily can be forcibly excluded from such competition, the likely consequence will be a heightened desire to evade the restriction. This desire is powerfully stimulated by advertising directed at the youth market from the makers and sellers of clothing. The first thing that uniformed schoolchildren do upon their return home from school is to change out of the clothes that denote low status and submission to authority and into clothes of their own choosing. Many will tell you they feel an instant uplift upon changing out of school clothes.

2) Class discrimination, i.e., snobbery, amongst students derives from class discrimination in the adult society. Students in, say, Australia or England, are acutely aware of each other's economic and social status, uniformity of school attire notwithstanding. They know who lives in a "good neighborhood" and who doesn't and whose family drives what kind of car. They are quicker than their multi-clad American counterparts to discriminate against classmates whose station in life is less privileged than their own. I am not claiming that the absence of school uniforms promotes tolerance, but rather that there is no evidence to show that their use curbs prejudice.

   Furthermore, since schools select distinctive uniforms, students attending a school serving an economically deprived neighborhood are instantly distinguishable from their more fortunate counterparts at the other end of town. Within a given school, uniform styles often denote a student's grade level, thus are more likely to promote, rather than reduce, rank-based bullying such has hazing and fagging.

Uniforms Do Not Reduce Gang Violence

3) The assumption that clothing is a factor contributing to gang violence is based on a naive notion of what motivates people to violent acts and to gang affiliation. The forcible substitu-

tion of officially-approved colors for gang colors during school hours does not address the root causes of youth violence nor does anything to impede the violence itself. In fact, the uniform may facilitate violence because its wearer's individual identity is subsumed by the group identity. Aren't the most dangerous mobs of all the ones that wear uniforms?

4) School uniforms are not economical. Students require two distinct, non-interchangeable sets of clothes. Manufacturers of school uniforms typically cooperate closely with the schools that use their product. This relationship, founded on a captive market, invites corruption. Not surprisingly, school uniforms, relative to mufti of equivalent quality, are more expensive. This is due in part to the relatively low production runs of a particular design. In response to the cost factor, some schools have a clothing pool consisting of donated old uniforms. However, a shabby, third-hand, ill-fitting uniform received gratis from the school clothing pool is an advertisement of its wearer's dependence on charity—the very thing uniforms are supposed to conceal.

In the United States, any attempt by public school authorities to require parents to obtain special clothing for their children will be perceived by at least a few people as an unwarranted intrusion by an agent of the government into areas of taste, personal choice and how free citizens spend, or don't spend, their dollars. It's hard to imagine that politicians would fail to anticipate the legal fall-out. Nevertheless, many of them, following the lead of President [Bill] Clinton, persist in touting the imaginary benefits of school uniforms—a placebo, cynically prescribed for the gullible.

School Uniforms Should Accommodate Muslim Culture

Fareena Alam

Fareena Alam, whose fight for the right to wear *hijab* (a head scarf often worn by Muslim women) in her British passport photo led to new rules in 2000, discusses Shabina Begum's highly publicized case to wear the *jilbab* (a long loose over-garment) as part of a school uniform. Alam agrees that Begum should be able to wear the jilbab, but disagrees with Begum's assessment that all Muslim women should dress like that as well. According to Alam, there is no such thing as "pure Islam, free of cultural baggage," and that Muslims can dress in a way that both conforms to Islamic law and accommodates local culture. Alam lives in London and is the editor of the Muslim magazine *Q-News*.

The fascinating thing about [the March 22, 2006] ruling against Shabina Begum as she fights to wear the jilbab in school is the ensuing diversity of Muslim opinion. Far from single-minded condemnation of the ruling, a surprisingly high number of Muslims seem to share the opinion of one ex-student from Denbigh high, who said: "I think it was best she lost. I went to the high school she caused problems for. They cater for Muslims by allowing baggy shalwar kameez [a long tunic worn over pants]."

Fareena Alam, "Style and Substance," *Guardian Unlimited*, March 22, 2006. http://comment isfree.guardian.co.uk. Reproduced by permission of Guardian News Service, LTD.

When this story first broke out, I wrote another piece because the obsession with preventing Muslim girls from exercising the—wait for it—freedom to choose what they want to wear was getting ridiculous—especially because the controversy surrounding the French ban on the hijab in schools was at its height then.

Muslim students dressed in school uniforms visit Malaysia's Kuala Lumpur City Centre.

I still defend Shabina's right to wear what she wants—my own out of court battle to wear hijab in my passport photograph led to a change in the Home Office rules in 2000.

I really believe this case could have been nipped in the bud by Denbigh high school. What is so offensive about the jilbab? The fact that the school insisted on challenging Shabina's initial victory in March 2005 in the highest court in the country reflects a kind of arrogance. However, part of the blame for this escalation surely also goes to Shabina and those advising her.

School Tried to Accommodate Muslim Students

Granted, the Muslim headmistress of Denbigh and her staff went to great lengths to accommodate the needs of the school's Muslim students. I vociferously defend Shabina's right to wear what she wants, but I cannot accept her argument that she must wear the jilbab because "nothing else is Islamic". What is popularly known as the jilbab today (and let's not assume this is automatically equivalent to the word "jilbab" mentioned in the Qur'an) is, I'm afraid, an Arab dress. An African or Malay or Chinese Muslim woman is likely to take offence, as I do, in the suggestion that she is not a pious enough Muslim because she does not wear the jilbab—or love houmus or cous cous or whatever.

Muslim women of all cultures have covered their bodies for centuries in ways that embody Islamic rulings while reflecting their local cultures and sense of style. Shabina is quoted on the BBC News website as having said: "I feel it is an obligation upon Muslim women to wear this [the jilbab], although there are many other opinions."

And yet, Shabina's seeming openness was absent when I was on the BBC World Service with her this afternoon. She said, and I so wish she hadn't, that "the shalwar khameez is not Islamic because the kameez (tunic) only comes to the knees, with the shalwar (the slacks) showing the size of one's legs." It is unfortunate that Shabina should express such disdain because, if we're going to nit-pick, I can pull out news clippings containing pictures of Shabina where the shape and size of her thigh were clear-

British Support for Ban on Veils

Percent of surveyed Britons who would support a ban on Muslim women wearing veils in school: **53 percent**

Taken from: "Survey Finds Support for Veil Ban," November 29, 2006. www.bbc.co.uk/.

ly discernible through her jilbab as she victoriously walked down the steps outside the courts a year ago [2005].

Tight enough, any dress, including the style of jilbabs worn by many, can show the shape of the body and, frankly, be quite sexy.

Islam Is Affected by Local Culture

For years, Muslims around me have said: "Islam must be separated from culture." While this slogan has deep and well-meaning roots—such as the struggle to teach people that honour killing, often justified with religious excuses, is a cultural practice that is unequivocally abhorred in Islam—the clash between culture and religion is ultimately a false one. This idea of a "pure Islam, free of cultural baggage" is a false one. Religion manifests itself in the realities of life. Must we all neutralise ourselves—even the aspects that do not contravene Islam, to be accepted as "pious"? What is this "one Islam" or "one voice" people call for, and who decides what it says?

A mosque in China, with its bright red and gold interior and pagoda-like exterior blends beautifully into its surroundings as does the new mosque in Bradford, made of the same local stone as the buildings around it; they are completely different but both sacred places of worship for Muslims.

"Like a crystal clear river, Islam and sacred law are pure but colourless, until they reflect the Chinese, African, and other bedrock over which they flow," wrote Dr Umar Faruq Abdallah, of the Nawawi Foundation in Chicago, USA, in his paper, "Islam and the Cultural Imperative."

Muslim reaction to Shabina's case reveals once again the ongoing debate and discussion taking place within British Islam. The same diversity—and confidence—was revealed in the Muslim outrage at the violent protests of their fellow brothers against the Danish cartoons. [In September, 2005, the Danish newspaper *Jyllands-Posten* published twelve editorial cartoons featuring the image of Muhammad. The purpose was to highlight the debate over how to reconcile free speech and religious law. Since portraying Muhammad is against Islamic law, the cartoons were deeply offensive to some people. The resulting uproar led to death threats, the burning of embassies, and riots.]

Young British Muslims are confidently expressing their views and taking ownership of the agenda and that can only be a good thing. In many ways, Shabina is one of them and I wish her all the best. She did what she felt she had to do. Her feistiness and single-minded determination is admirable, even if it was perhaps misguided at times.

Ultimately, I salute her for using the legal and democratic means available to her as a citizen of this country. It hasn't been a total loss; she won many little victories on the way.

What You Should Know About Dress Codes in Schools

Dress Codes in the United States

- Dress code and school uniform policies are becoming more common.

- In 2007, 34 percent more schools were using uniforms than the previous year.

- In 1997 only 3 percent of public schools required school uniforms.

- In 2001, 12 percent of public schools required school uniforms.

- In 2007 one in four public elementary schools and one in eight public middle and high schools in the United States had policies dictating what a student wears to school.

- Uniforms were first adopted by private schools who were following the British tradition of school uniforms.

- The use of school uniforms rose after President Bill Clinton recommended them in his 1996 State of the Union speech. Clinton stated, "If it means that teenagers will stop killing each other over designer jackets, then our public schools should require their students to wear uniforms."

- More than one-third of children aged 12–14 dislike wearing school uniforms versus only 14 percent of children aged 5–8 years.

The Effects of Dress Codes in Schools

- Mandatory school uniforms gained favor in public schools after schools in Long Beach, California, had successful results from adopting uniforms. The school district reported that after adopting a mandatory uniform policy, fights went down 51 percent and sex offenses dropped by 74 percent.

- Analysis of subsequent studies have not shown that dress codes or uniforms have any effect on student performance or behavior.

- School administrators in districts with a dress code are more apt to believe that the dress codes positively affect student performance and behavior.

- A 2000 survey of the National Association of Elementary School Principals reported that 67 percent of principals in schools with uniforms saw an improvement in their students' concentration level, 62 percent saw a positive effect on school safety, and 40 percent believed uniforms helped to improve attendance.

Who Has Dress Codes?

- No states mandate school uniforms.

- Twenty-one states and the District of Columbia authorize local districts to require students to wear uniforms.

- Uniforms have been most popular in the South, and the states that have the highest percentage of students who wear uniforms are Texas and Louisiana.

- Of public schools with a school uniform policy, about 75 percent have mandatory policies and 25 percent have voluntary policies.

- Uniforms are more likely to be required in schools with a high percentage of students eligible for free or reduced-price lunches (11 percent in schools with 75 percent or more free or reduced-price lunch eligibility) compared with schools in which less than 50 percent of students were eligible (2 percent or less).

- Schools with 50 percent or more minority enrollment are more likely to require student uniforms than those with lower minority enrollment (13 percent compared with 2 percent or less).

Dress Codes and the Law

- Most lawsuits against school dress codes fail. Judges usually decide that the policies do not suppress free speech.

- The issue of dress codes and school uniforms has not come before the Supreme Court.

- Often it is parents rather than students who organize protests against proposed dress codes.

- Some of the most active and organized students to fight dress codes have been "Goths," who object to what they see as suppression of their right to free expression.

- In 1996 a proposed dress code for teachers in Santa Ana, California, set off a yearlong battle between the school board and the union. The courts determined that the board could set a teacher dress code.

- In 1998 a bill went before the Maryland legislature requiring school boards to set teacher dress codes. The bill did not pass.

Dress Codes and Cost

- In 2004 sales of school uniforms rose to $1.5 billion.

- In 2006 parents expected to pay about $233 on school uniforms, per child.

- Uniforms are most often purchased at department stores.

- Parents actually spent an average of $162 per child on school uniforms.

What You Should Do About Dress Codes in Schools

Since the issue of school dress codes remains contentious, public opinion can still play a big part in whether school districts decide to start—or stop—a dress code. Officials in the Long Beach Unified School District in Long Beach, California, say that the reason they began their influential school uniform policy was because parents asked for one. By contrast, in 2007, after fielding numerous complaints from parents, the school board in Hamburg, Arkansas, voted to stop requiring students to wear uniforms. And the battles continue. As this book went to press, students in the Marketing Department at Illinois State University were fighting a dress code that applied only to marketing students.

Clearly, dress codes are an issue in flux. And the courts seem to be just as confused as the school districts. The Supreme Court has never ruled on the issue of dress codes. The case most often cited on the issue is 1969's *Tinker v. Des Moines Independent Community School District*, which involved students' rights to wear black armbands. The Court ruled that the students could wear the armbands unless they caused substantial disruption or invaded the rights of others. Ironically, both proponents and opponents of dress codes cite this case to further their arguments. Proponents of dress codes note that the judges specifically noted that their ruling did not apply to "the length of skirts or type of clothing." Opponents argue that the case reinforced students' right to expression through clothing. Smaller courts around the country have ruled both in favor of dress codes and against them. With no clear precedent set, students have more power to influence school districts' policies.

The first step in influencing policy is to find like-minded people. Start talking about the issues with parents, teachers, and friends. Gather these people into a core group who would be willing to fight with you. A small group is not a problem. Many people do not pay attention to local politics, so just a few voices can make a big difference. The old maxim of the squeaky wheel getting the grease is especially applicable to issues with the school board.

Research Your Subject

Before coming up with a plan of action, check the Internet. Dozens of organizations have sprung up to fight or support dress codes. When using a search engine, try words like "standard school attire," "mandatory uniforms," or "students fight (or support) dress code." Some of these groups are still active and some lost—or won— their battles years ago. Read about these groups and see how they fought for their position. Even groups that failed can give you ideas on what not to do. If a group is still active, feel free to contact them. They could offer you good advice or point to additional resources. A particularly sympathetic group might even offer you help in your own efforts.

The next step is to become an expert on your subject. Again, the Internet is an invaluable resource. Learn about districts that have adopted dress codes and what the results have been. Check the existing research. The studies on dress codes have not been especially definitive, so no matter what your position, there is respectable research to back you up. On the pro-dress-code side of the debate, Long Beach Unified School District has some compelling research (www.lbschools.net) touting its success with uniforms. On the anti-dress-code side, David Brunsma is a recognized expert (http://sociology.missouri.edu/New%20Website%20WWW/Faculty%20and%20Staff/David_Brunsma.htm) in debunking dress code benefits.

Get Your Position Heard

After arming yourself with facts, the next step is to get your position heard. Brainstorm with your group on the best ways to do this and what each person is willing to do. Find out where each group member's talents lie. Have your members bring up the issue to friends and neighbors. Pass petitions around, speak at school board meetings, and write letters to the editor of the local paper and school paper. Give your group a memorable name, and make the group noticeable by issuing press releases to the media on official letterhead. Write an editorial for the local paper and sign it with your name, mentioning your affiliation with the group. Create a Web presence with an appealing, professional-looking Web site. Think of ways to attract media attention. Local TV stations like to cover contentious issues like dress codes, and if you can think of an appealing event, the station will likely send a reporter to cover it. Think visually. Humorous events and demonstrations are more likely to appeal to television stations than dry meetings. Make sure you call the station in advance to give them time to put it into their schedule.

No matter how passionate you are about your issue, you need to remember to always present your case in a calm, professional manner. School boards respond well to reasoned arguments and compelling facts (as well as public pressure). If school dress codes are something you feel strongly about, your position is worth fighting for because your efforts can make a big difference in shaping public opinion.

The editors have compiled the following list of organizations concerned with the issues debated in this book. The descriptions are derived from materials provided by the organizations. All have publications or information available for interested readers. The list was compiled on the date of publication of the present volume; the information provided here may change. Be aware that many organizations take several weeks or longer to respond to inquiries, so allow as much time as possible.

American Civil Liberties Union (ACLU)
125 Broad St., 18th Floor, New York, NY 10004
(212) 549-2500 • toll-free: (888) 567-ACLU
e-mail: membership@aclu.org
Web site: www.aclu.org

The ACLU champions the rights set forth in the Bill of Rights of the U.S. Constitution: freedom of speech, press, assembly, and religion; due process of law and fair trial; equality before the law regardless of race, color, sexual orientation, national origin, political opinion, or religious belief. They conduct activities including litigation, advocacy, and public education.

The Center for First Amendment Rights, Inc. (CFAR)
90 Statehouse Sq., 13th Floor, Hartford, CT 06103-3708
(860) 541-3339
e-mail: info@cfarfreedom.org
Web site: www.cfarfreedom.org

CFAR is dedicated to increasing the understanding and appreciation of the First Amendment of the U.S. Constitution among students and the general public, particularly in Connecticut and

New England. CFAR provides educational programming and also serves as a resource center for First Amendment issues and information.

The Coalition for Student & Academic Rights (CO-STAR)
PO Box 491, Solebury, PA 18963
(215) 862-9096
e-mail: info@co-star.org
Web site: www.co-star.org

CO-STAR is a nonprofit network of lawyers who help college students and professors with legal problems. Their primary goal is to educate the academic community about the law and their rights. The Web site provides links to other resources for students.

Education Commission of the States (ECS)
700 Broadway, #1200, Denver, CO 80203-3460
(303) 299-3600
e-mail: ecs@ecs.org
Web site: www.ecs.org

The mission of the Education Commission of the States is to help states develop effective policy and practice for public education by providing data, research, analysis, and leadership, and by facilitating collaboration, the exchange of ideas among the states, and long-range strategic thinking. The Web site provides information on current issues, as well as links to policy briefs, newsletters, and periodicals.

The Freechild Project
PO Box 6185, Olympia, WA 98507-6185
(360) 753-2686
e-mail: info@freechild.org
Web site: www.freechild.org

The Freechild Project's mission is to advocate, inform, and celebrate social change led by and with young people around the world, particularly those who have been historically denied the right to participate. The Freechild Project believes it is completely unethical to exclude young people from participating in the actions that affect them most. Consequently, they work to engage young people in critical democratic action centered on growing community, culture, and society. The organization publishes a newsletter that is available on the Web site.

National School Boards Association (NSBA)
1680 Duke St., Alexandria, VA 22314
(703) 838-6722
e-mail: info@nsba.org
Web site: www.nsba.org/

NSBA advocates local school boards as the ultimate expression of grassroots democracy. NSBA supports the capacity of each school board to envision the future of education in its community, to establish a structure and environment that allow all students to reach their maximum potential, to provide accountability for the community on performance in the schools, and to serve as the key community advocate for children and youth and their public schools.

The National Youth Rights Association (NYRA)
1133 19th St. NW, 9th Floor, Washington, DC 20036
(202) 833-1200, x5714
e-mail: nyra@youthrights.org
Web site: www.youthrights.org

The NYRA defends the civil and human rights of young people in the United States through educating people about youth rights, working with public officials, and empowering young people to work on their own behalf. They believe certain basic rights are intrinsic parts of American citizenship and transcend age or status limits.

Underground Action Alliance
PO Box 7591, Pittsburgh, PA 15213-9998
e-mail: info@undergroundactionalliance.org
Web site: undergroundactionalliance.org

Underground Action Alliance encourages members of the punk-rock community to assume the critical role of citizen-activist. Citizen-activists speaks for those who have not found their voice, seek out and listen to those whose voices have been ignored or silenced, and empower their community to advocate for itself and work for justice. The Students' Rights Resource is devoted to educating American students about their constitutional rights and how to exercise and protect them in public schools.

BIBLIOGRAPHY

Books

David L. Brunsma, *The School Uniform Movement and What It Tells Us About American Education*. Lanham, MD: Rowman and Littlefield, 2004.

———, *Uniforms in Public Schools: A Decade of Research and Debate*. Lanham, MD: Rowman and Littlefield, 2005.

Jennifer Criak, *Uniforms Exposed: From Conformity to Transgression*. Gordonsville, VA: Berg, 2005.

Paul Fussell, *Uniforms: Why We Are What We Wear*. Boston: Houghton Mifflin, 2002.

Sandra Harris, *Best Practices of Award-Winning Elementary School Principals*. Thousand Oaks, CA: Corwin, 2005.

Kathleen A. Hempelman, *Teen Legal Rights*, Westport, CT: Greenwood, 2000.

Ruth P. Rubenstein, *Dress Codes: Meanings and Messages in American Culture*. Boulder, CO: Westview, 2001.

Traci Truly, *Teen Rights (and Responsibilities)*. Naperville, IL: Sphinx, 2005.

Periodicals

Demian Bulwa, "Studies Divided on Effects of School Uniforms," *San Francisco Chronicle*, March 27, 2007.

Laura Clark, "School Uniform Improves Pupils' Behaviour Both In and Out of School," *Daily Mail*, July 10, 2007.

Claudia Gryvatz Copquin, "School Uniforms Should Replace Improper Attire," *Newsday*, September 14, 2007.

Megan Downs, "Students Want More Expression," *Florida Today*, September 27, 2007. www.floridatoday.com.

Dave Groves, "Dress Code Fails; Will Uniforms Fly at High Schools?" *Oakland Press*, July 18, 2007.

Brian Hennigan, "Absurd School Uniform Claim Leaves a Nazi Taste," *Scotsman*, January 16, 2007. http://news.scotsman.com.

Kristine Hughes, "Districts on Teacher Dress: Have Some Class," *Dallas Morning News*, September 15, 2006.

John Karas, "Parents, Students See Red over Dress Code," *East Hartford Gazette*, July 18, 2007. www.zwire.com.

Samantha Long, "Student's Take on Standard School Attire: Don't Pile on More Stress and Expense on Kids and Families," *Tennessean*, April 1, 2007.

Michelle McPeters, "Parent's Take on Standard School Attire: It Will Clear Away the Clutter of Ridicule," *Tennessean*, April 1, 2007.

Omuyonga Okata, "Why I Still Love My Primary School Uniform," *Kenya Times*, March 19, 2006.

Jamie Reid, "Beaumont Students Find 'Loopholes' in Dress Codes to Add Splashes of Individuality," *Beaumont Enterprise*, September 9, 2007. www.southeasttexaslive.com.

Celia Rivenbark, "Uniforms: Soul-Sucking Sameness," *Jewish World Review*, September 12, 2006.

George Royal, "What Is the Point of School Uniforms?" *EzineArticles* 23, May 21, 2007. http://ezinearticles.com.

David Ryan, "Dress Code Goes Up on Appeal," *Napa Valley Register*, July 19, 2007.

Dorit Sasson, "Children's School Uniforms: Pros and Cons for a Children's Dress Code at School," *Suite 101*, April 22, 2007. http://newteachersupport.suite101.com.

Steve Schedin, "York City Schools Nix Middle-School Uniforms," *York Daily Record*, July 20, 2007. www.ydr.com.

Pete Sherman, "Parents Resisting School Uniforms," *State Journal-Register*, September 13, 2007. www.sj-r.com.

Bridie Smith, "No Skirting Teacher Dress Code," *The Age*, July 18, 2007. www.theage.com.au.

Nancy Steinbach, "Students Do Not Always Like Being Told What to Wear (Duh!)" *Voice of America*, July 11, 2007. www.voanews.com.

Joe Sylvester, "Cheerleader Uniforms Don't Meet Dress Code," *Times-Tribune.com*, September 20, 2007. www.thetimes-tribune.com.

Luanne Traud, "Thou Shall Not Show Cleavage," *Roanoke Times*, July 11, 2007. www.roanoke.com.

INDEX